HORSES *help* HEROES

ONE THOUSAND MILES NON STOP CHALLENGE

Horses Help Heroes and RPM
Photography by Adam De Silva / RPM

RPM
Bell Pottinger Group
DIAGEO

HHH Books
Swan Yard, West Market Place,
Cirencester, Gloucestershire
GL7 2NH

Tel: 0128 564 1305
www.horseshelpheroes.org.uk

First published in 2011

Design and layout, RPM Ltd London
www.rpmltd.com

ISBN: 978-0-9571181-0-2

Printed and Bound in England by Precision Printing, 47 Thames Road, Barking, IG11 OHQ
Copies of the book may be purchased from the Publisher HHH Books
Cover Price £20.00 Postage and packing £4.00

NOTE: Proceeds from the sale of this book are for the benefit of Horses Help Heroes Fund Raising

Introduction

Horses Help Heroes is a campaign to raise substantial funds to deliver direct practical support to seriously wounded members of the British armed forces. These numbers continue to increase, and for every publicised active service fatality there are often many others with horrific injuries.

The campaign was the inspiration of 'Jacks' El Tawil, a Wiltshire-based paramedic with a lifelong passion for horses. The fundraising focus was a challenge for a team of seriously wounded servicemen to drive a horse-drawn replica WW1 ambulance non-stop, day and night, for a thousand miles - Land's End to John O'Groats - in less than 10 days.

Under the umbrella of Help for Heroes, money raised will also be shared with other military charities including ABF The Soldiers' Charity, Combat Stress and BLESMA - British Limbless Ex Servicemen's Association.

Support has been nothing short of magnificent. A letter of great encouragement from HRH The Duke of Cambridge. Generous help to enable them to attend many prestigious equestrian and military events including National Hunt, Flat Racing, Eventing, Show Jumping, Polo, Pony Club, Carriage Driving, Dressage, and Country and Military Shows.

After initially describing the challenge as an act of madness, the British Driving Society gave enormous support and advice. The challenge began on a sunny day in Land's End on June 21st 2011. Many smiles, "good lucks", tears, laughs, long days and even longer nights later, the team arrived in John O'Groats having raised significant funds.

The team included 46 disparate, highly individual volunteers, most of whom had never met before; 7 horseboxes; 21 horses; numerous vehicles and a replica WW1 ambulance. At times on the journey the rolling 24-hour caravan extended 80 miles from end to end. A substantial number of homes, stables, fields and food was offered up for the horses and the team to recharge - often at very short notice. Heart-warming generosity was universal.

The vast majority of the photographs of the challenge were taken by Adam De Silva whose services were kindly donated by marketing agency RPM, our main sponsor. Adam writes, "Every day I saw happiness, sadness, moments of reflection and relationships pushed to the test. Most of all, I saw a group of people including 7 injured ex-servicemen work together and share one goal: to overcome adversity and accomplish something."

The challenge was completed in 8 days and 7 hours.

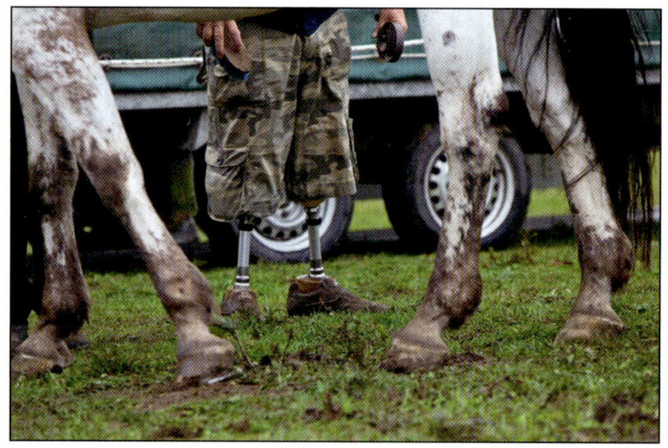

ST JAMES'S PALACE

As a Nation, we are quick to recognise the selflessness and dedication of our men and women in uniform and, tragically, the sacrifice they are sometimes called upon to make on our behalf. So many people in recent years have come forward wanting to do something to help. It has been magnificent and, frankly, made me feel very proud to be British. Occasionally, however, a few have come up with ideas of such originality that they stick out from the crowd. Horses Help Heroes is one of these rare initiatives.

To carriage drive a pair of horses the length of Great Britain, continuously for ten days, combines in one the great British traits of thirst for adventure, support and compassion for our wounded soldiers, sailors and airmen, and a love of horses – with just the mildest sprinkling of healthy eccentricity.

Under the banner of Help for Heroes, Horses Help Heroes aims to provide financial and emotional support to those Servicemen and women and their families who are most in need. I salute all those involved with Horses Help Heroes for their tireless commitment, energy and originality in their drive toward this vision. I urge everyone to support them, in whatever way they can.

William

Our Charities

The campaign aims to raise substantial funds to provide direct personal support to those seriously damaged, physically or mentally, servicemen and women and their families who are in need. This need is increasing strongly as the number of our wounded is growing significantly.

We are operating under the umbrella of the Help for Heroes charity and money raised will be used by its Quick Reaction Fund to respond rapidly to wherever needs are most necessary. In addition, Help for Heroes has agreed to allocate Horses Help Heroes funds to other charities that might include:
www.helpforheroes.org.uk

Long established, The Soldiers' Charity gives lifetime support, whatever the problem, whenever needed. Requests for assistance from The Soldiers' Charity have grown by 30% since 2005 and funds must increase to continue to meet the demands on its valuable support.
www.soldierscharity.org

British Limbless Ex Servicemen Association is a membership organisation that supports ex-servicemen and women who have lost limbs or the use of their limbs. Support is provided to their members' rehabilitation through activities such as sailing, skiing etc; a national welfare network gives support and advice, and 2 nursing homes provide residential and respite care.
www.blesma.org

The leading military charity specialising in the care of veterans' mental health related to their service career. Since 2009, the numbers of the ex-servicemen and women who have made contact has risen by 72% to over 4,400 current cases. On average, veterans delay seeking help by 13 years after their active service.
www.combatstress.org.uk

The inspiration behind Horses Help Heroes is 'Jacks' El Tawil who is no stranger to challenges and has always been besotted with horses.

She left school at 16 without 'O' levels. In her early years, most of her time was spent helping in stables, then working as a groom, a mother's help with a family for 10 years, and then running a mobile catering business.

Her equestrian and other achievements have all been developed in her spare time. Jacks broke Packers Hill who jumped a 7ft 4" wall at Aachen, Holland; bought a 3 year-old gelding, Jued Lad, with her insurance money and then sold him as an eventer to the Swedish team for the 1990 World Championships; broke her neck in 4 places while Europe's top female 350cc motorbike racer; taught pony club children; became a Wiltshire paramedic, and drives carriages for weddings and funerals.

As a mother of 3 sons, how did she come to be driving her girls 'Molly' and ' Rosie' in a WWI ambulance 1000 miles - all for charity?

Jacks is a Wiltshire NHS paramedic with 17 years experience. In recent years, she mentored army technician medics to improve frontline response times for 'IV drugs and fluids' before they went to Afghanistan or Iraq. She also often sees service people on their return in paramedic situations, tackling the inevitable post-front issues, or meeting their families when they don't return or are hospitalised. Through this, Jacks came to see and understand the increasing number of wounded personnel who need costly support to recover from the horrific physical and mental injuries inflicted by war.

Having experienced this first-hand, Jacks was inspired to raise funds directly for the individuals and their families. So on her 50th birthday, the idea was born. It had to involve horses, as they are her life, and what could be more fitting than using her own

horses to pull a WW1 ambulance driven by a team of seriously wounded soldiers – all in aid of raising desperately needed funds?

The commitment Jacks has shown this year far exceeds that of the '8-day challenge' itself. She has attended more than 40 events, covered thousands of miles and exhausted many more hours, and yet as we go to print she continues her tireless dedication to raising funds. She is a 'workhorse' - an inspiration.

WOUNDED MEN

Matt Wilson, Born in 1976, Matt joined the Army in 2005, choosing the Rifles Regiment. After serving in Iraq and Kosovo, he went to Afghanistan, where, in spring 2009, he stepped on a pressure pad for a roadside bomb. He lost his left leg and severely injured his right arm. After a lengthy recuperation, Matt has made a good recovery. Now discharged from the army, he is considering his future career plans. Matt had to learn to ride and carriage drive for the challenge and has been a very active participator in our fundraising events.

Colin Hamilton, Sergeant Colin Hamilton is a serving soldier with 3 SCOTS and based near Inverness. He joined the army in 1993 with the Royal Highland Fusiliers, transferring to The Black Watch in 2001 as a Warrior vehicle Commander serving in Kosovo and Iraq. While on duty in Kosovo, he went to the rescue of a colleague who was entangled in a high-voltage electric cable. As a result, Colin's right leg was so badly damaged that it had to be amputated above the knee. His prosthetic leg is at the cutting edge of developments in electronic movement of the knee, ankle and foot - one of only 12 in the world. He intends to stay in 3 SCOTS. Colin had to learn to ride and carriage drive for the challenge.

Danny Holmes, Danny served in the Life Guards from 1983-1994 mainly in Windsor and North Germany, but he also served in Iraq in the first Gulf War from 1990-91 with 7 Armoured Brigade (The Desert Rats). Danny has lost his right leg and had to learn to carriage drive for the challenge. He now works in children's care services. He sees helping with the fundraising part of the challenge and a chance to repay some of the benefits that he has received from service charities.

Dr Francis Atkinson, Born in 1981, Francis Atkinson joined the army as a doctor on completion of his medical degree. Currently a member of 16 Medical Regiment, Royal Army Medical Corps, Francis was posted to Afghanistan in 2010 to provide medical cover in a Forward Operating Base. While on patrol he was shot in his right arm, losing all function of the hand and wrist. Francis is currently undergoing surgery, but hopes to resume his career as an army medical officer before too long. Francis had to learn to ride and carriage drive (with one hand) for the challenge and provided back-up to the paramedics.

Captain Charlie Dalziel, Charlie attended Sandhurst, commissioning as an Officer in September 2007. He joined 1 SCOTS, The Royal Regiment of Scotland, and served in Iraq and Afghanistan. While on patrol in Afghanistan he was attending to a wounded Afghan soldier when he was shot through his right calf, shattering the tibia and the fibula. Charlie is on the road to recovery. He is unlikely to be able to resume frontline duties, but continues with his regiment. Charlie had to learn to ride and carriage drive for the challenge, but was unable to participate due to medical treatment.

Mick Foulds, Born in 1952 in London, Mick joined the Territorial Army in 1976, serving with the Royal Corps of Transport and subsequently the Royal Engineers until 1983 in Germany, Cyprus and Denmark. Mick is a double amputee, having lost both legs below the knee, and had to learn to carriage drive for the challenge. However, riding is something he does on his own horses, and he is a keen player of Polocrosse. Mick devotes much of his time to fundraising, counselling and supporting BLESMA colleagues.

Ed Addington, As a Captain in the 2nd Rifles, Ed was serving in Afghanistan when his armoured vehicle was blown up. Both his legs were severely damaged and their recovery is proving to be slow. So far, he has undergone 20 operations and the prognosis remains uncertain. Ed is currently returned to university studies. He had to learn to ride and carriage drive for the challenge, but unfortunately was not medically able to do the challenge.

Paul Burns, Born in 1961, Paul joined The Parachute Regiment as a junior soldier aged 16. After training, he was posted to 2 PARA in Berlin, before moving with them to Northern Ireland in 1979. In August that year, his vehicle was blown up by a roadside bomb planted by the IRA at Warren Point; Paul was one of two survivors, the other six crew members dying in the blast. He suffered severe injuries and extensive burns, including amputation of his left leg. Paul is very active and devotes much of his time to fundraising in a range of activities to assist injured colleagues through BLESMA. He had to learn to ride and carriage drive for the challenge.

John Sandford Hart, Served in Royal Electrical and Mechanical Engineers, leaving in 1989. John is an amputee and has committed a great deal of time to service charities, having achieved several entries in the Guinness Book of Records, including the fastest London marathon on crutches. John is continuously raising funds for military charities, participating in major physical challenges. He runs 2 of his own businesses in house building and hiring and driving limousines. He had to learn to ride and carriage drive for the challenge.

BUILDING THE AMBULANCE

Rob Shore - Expert conversion of the carriage to the replica WW1 ambulance

Rob's arm - Rob working with traditional tools

A horse-drawn brake was bought from Mark Broadbent of Fenix Carriages and this was converted into a replica WW1 ambulance by the expert workmanship of Rob Shore, with Darren Slade helping with the painting. Rob largely used typical traditional 19th century hand woodworking tools in this for a high-quality outcome. The ambulance is based on an original vehicle held by the Army Medical Services Museum at Keogh Barracks, Aldershot.

Darren painting

Guy Parry dressing the Ambulance banner

LONDON LAUNCH

Before the Changing of the Guard in Knightsbridge Barracks - Jacks and Matt

Capt Charlie Dalziel and Cpl Matt Wilson in front of Horse Guards Parade

Lord Strathclyde, Leader of the House of Lords, and James Gray MP outside the House of Lords

A contrastingly warm welcome from Chelsea Pensioners outside the Royal Hospital

FUNDRAISING BEFORE THE CHALLENGE

London International Horse Show Olympia

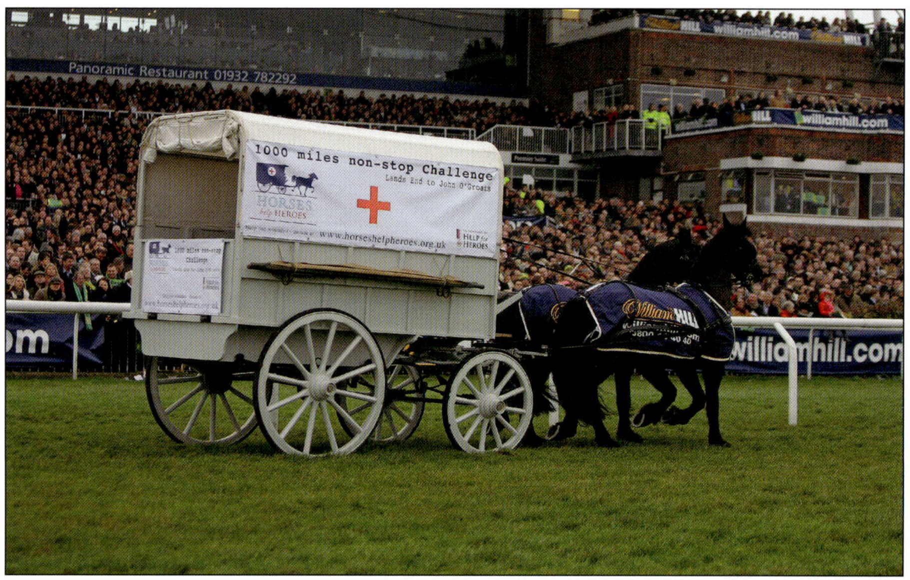

Parading at Kempton

King George VI Chase, Kempton. Sophie, Molly and Rosie

John Smith's Grand National - Matt up front

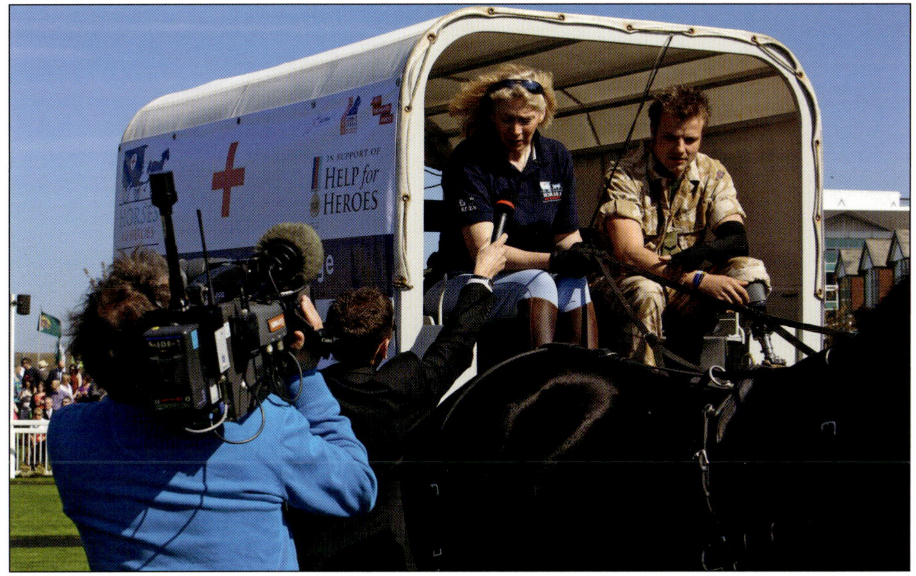

John Smith's Grand National - TV interviews

John Smith's Grand National - In the paddock at Aintree

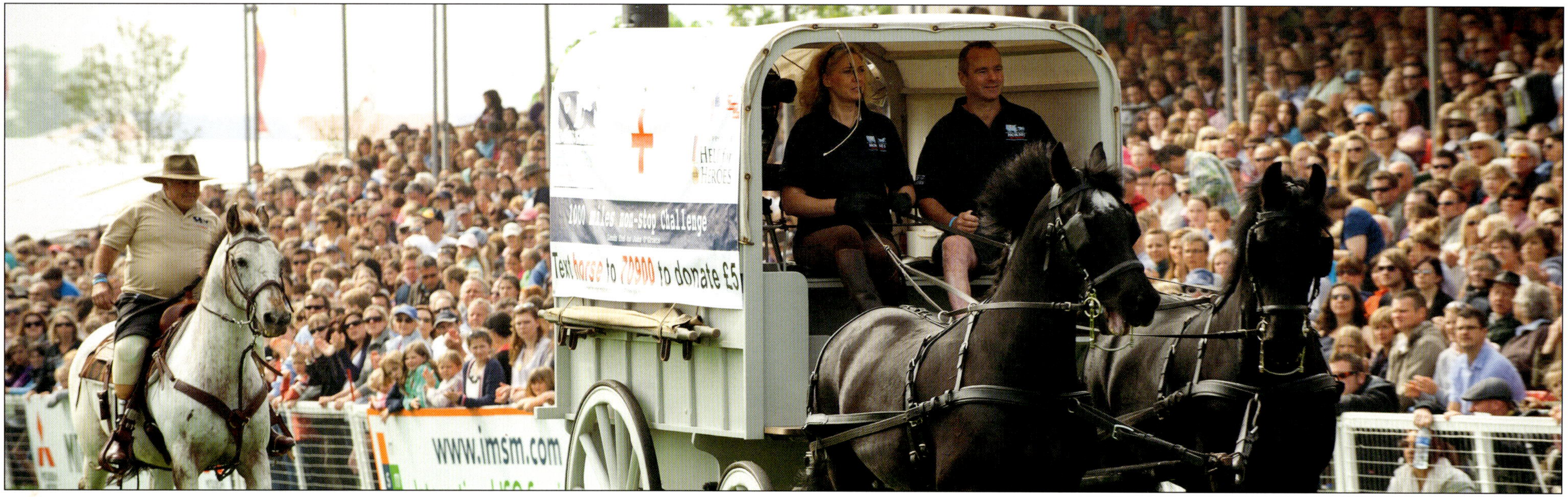

Badminton Horse Trials - Jacks and Paul followed by Mick on Kaz in main arena

Badminton Horse Trials

Mark Todd, Badminton champion 2011 - Wearing signed shirt donated to HHH

Newmarket 2000 Guineas

Newbury Farmers Market set up

Chester Festival

24-hour Rehersal - Stallions surge up Fish Hill, Gloucestershire

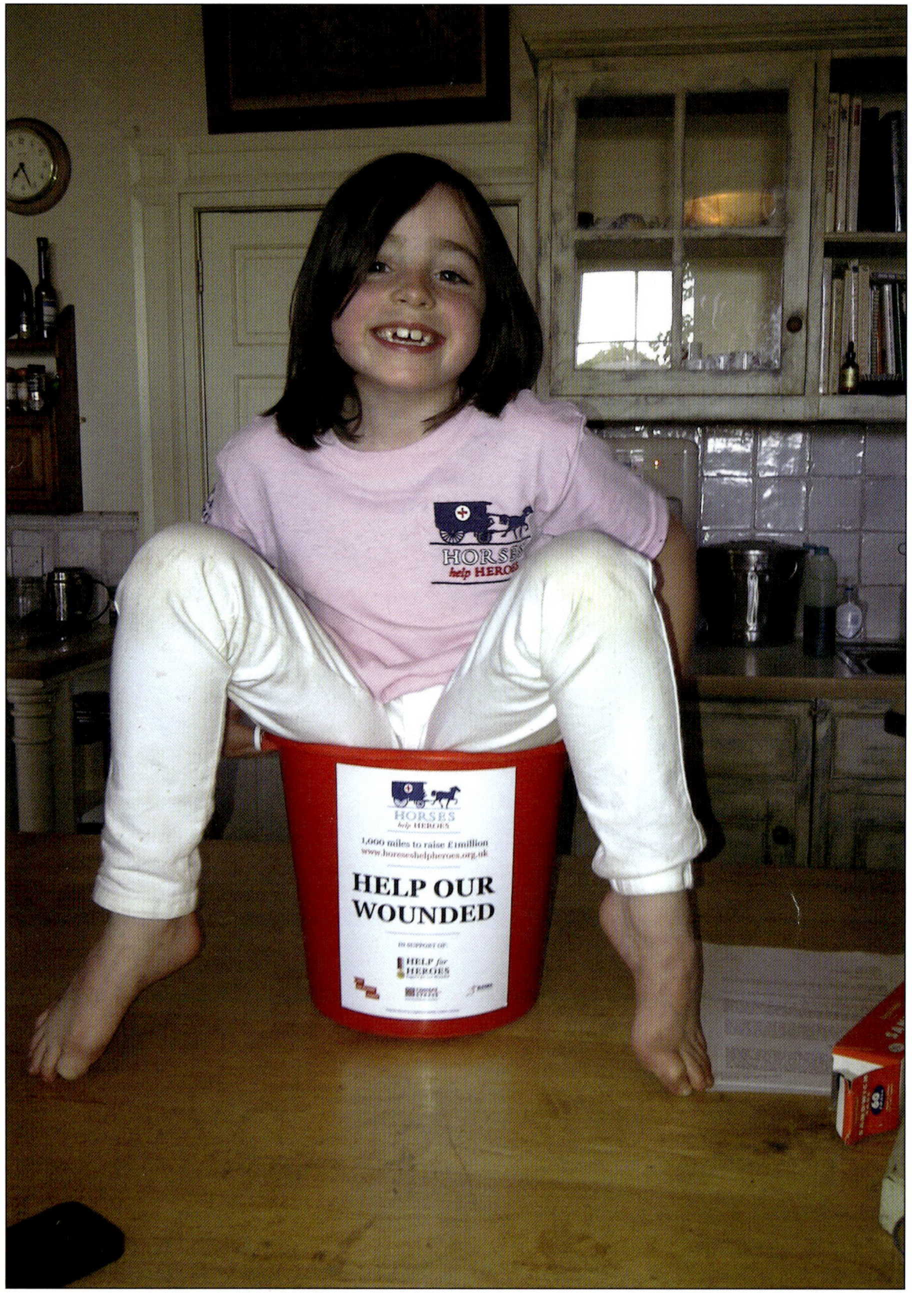

Violet at Hatton Country Fair

Beaufort International Polo and Country Fair

Steam rally

The Investec Epsom Derby Festival - Investec Horses Help Heroes Stake Race

The Investec Epsom Derby Festival - Adam and Harry El Tawil bucket collectors

The Investec Epsom Derby Festival -

Our smiling fundraisers on Derby Day

Winning owner, trainer and jockey receiving the trophy - Cpl Matt Wilson on the podium

Cpl Matt Wilson

TRAINING THE DRIVERS AND RIDERS

Helen puts Matt through his paces

Danny under instruction

Mick mounting Kaz

Mark Todd joins the group for the day

Ed makes brilliant progress

BBC Points West film training day at Helen Cole's Equestrian Centre

Driving lessons for Mick, John, Ed and Matt at sunset

Mayor of Penzance with Jacks El Tawil and The Team of Wounded Servicemen

Initial briefing from James Emson - Trennuggo Farm, Land's End

Tim Villiers further briefing

Henry Meakin and the Lady Mayor of Penzance

Phil Scott's Moulton Transport horse box sampling the Cornish mud

Henry receiving cheques at Trennuggo Farm BBQ with host Robert Eddie, on the right

Colin Hamilton, Mick Foulds and Jacks sharing plans at the BBQ

Former Household Cavalry Men reminisce

Live music from a trailer in the dry

THE ROUTE

Route	Place	ETA	Leg Mileage	Cumulative Mileage
Tuesday 21 June				
Start	Land's End	0900 hrs		0.0
A30	Penzance	1036 hrs	8.0	8.0
	Redruth	1430 hrs	19.6	27.6
	Indian Queens	1800 hrs	17.4	45.0
	Bodmin	2036 hrs	13.0	58.0
Wednesday 22 June				
A30	Launceston	0040 hrs	20.2	78.2
	Okehampton	0445 hrs	20.5	98.7
	Cheriton Bishop	0635 hrs	10.9	109.6
	Exeter	0820-0850 hrs	10.4	120.0
	Honiton	1220-1240 hrs	17.6	137.6
	Newcott	1340 hrs	6.6	144.2
B3170	Taunton	1700-1730 hrs	20.8	165.0
A358 / A378	Curry Rivel	1930 hrs	12.3	177.3
A372	Langport	1950 hrs	2.2	179.5
A37	Podimore	2115-2230 hrs	9.3	188.8
Thursday 23 June				
A37	Shepton Mallet	0230-0245 hrs	14.8	203.6
A367	Radstock	0515-0530 hrs	9.4	213.0
A4	Bath	0800-0830 hrs	9.2	222.2
	Chippenham	1045-1100 hrs	13.3	235.5
A429	Malmesbury	1300-1315 hrs	9.9	245.4
A435	Cirencester	1500-1515 hrs	9.6	255.0
	Cheltenham	1900-1920 hrs	36.4	291.4
A40	Gloucester	2110-2130 hrs	9.4	300.8
B4215	Newent	2320-2335 hrs	9.4	310.2
Friday 24 June				
A4127	Preston Cross	0100 hrs	7.0	317.2
A417	Hope Under Dinmore	0425 hrs	17.2	334.4
A49	Leominster	0600 hrs	5.8	340.2
	Ludlow	0800-0815 hrs	11.5	351.7
	Craven Arms	0930-0940 hrs	7.8	359.5
	Little Stretton	1040 hrs	6.2	365.7
	Church Stretton	1050-1105 hrs	1.7	367.4
	All Stretton Yew Tree Pub	1140-1155 hrs	3.1	370.5
	Shrewsbury	1330-1350 hrs	10.0	380.5
	Whitchurch	1710-1720 hrs	20.1	400.6
	Tarporley	2000-2020 hrs	14.4	415.0
	Warrington	2350-2400 hrs	18.6	433.6

Saturday 25 June				
A49	Ashton in Makerfield	0130 hrs	7.5	451.1
	Wigan	0300 hrs	5.9	457.0
	Leyland	0545 hrs	13.7	470.7
	Preston	0700 hrs	6.3	479.4
A6	Lancaster	1320 hrs	25.7	505.1
A6 / A6070	Carnforth	1500 hrs	8.3	513.4
A6070 / A65	Kendal	1815 hrs	16.3	529.7
A6	Shap	2130 hrs	16.4	546.1
	Penrith	2400 hrs	15.0	561.1
Sunday 26 June				
A6	Carlisle	0240 hrs	21.8	582.9
A7	Longtown	0340 hrs	8.4	591.3
A6071	Gretna	0415 hrs	4.8	596.1
B7076	Lockerbie	0615-0625 hrs	16.0	612.1
A702	Crawford	0955-1005 hrs	30.1	642.2
B7078	Abington	1030 hrs	3.3	645.5
	Kirkmuirhill	1230 hrs	16.6	662.1
A72 / A724	Glasgow	1600-2000 hrs	24.1	686.2
Monday 27 June				
A82	Dumbarton	2300-2310 hrs	19.9	706.1
	Renton	2345 hrs	2.9	709.0
	Tyndrum	0740-0750 hrs	39.6	748.6
A85	Dalmally	1020-1030 hrs	12.4	761.0
	Taynuilt	1250-1300 hrs	11.8	772.8
A828	Portnacroish	1710-1720 hrs	20.7	793.5
	North Ballachulish	1955-2005 hrs	13.0	806.5
A82	Fort William	2300-2315 hrs	12.5	819.0
Tuesday 28 June				
A82	Spean Bridge	0145 hrs	8.9	827.9
	Invergarry	0455 hrs	15.7	843.6
	Fort Augustus	0625-0635 hrs	7.5	851.1
	Drumndrochit	0945-1000 hrs	19.2	870.3
	Inverness	1230-1300 hrs	14.2	884.5
A9	Alness	1620-1630 hrs	20.3	904.8
	Tain	1900-1915 hrs	14.4	919.2
Wednesday 29 June				
A9	Brora	2225-2240 hrs	22.7	941.9
	Helmsdale	0055 hrs	11.4	953.3
	Dunbeath	0350 hrs	14.7	968.0
A99	Wick	0800-0830 hrs	20.5	988.5
	John O'Groats	1030 hrs	16.3	1004.8

Jacks with Molly and Rosie move to the famous start line

Trennuggo Farm farrier Robert comes to the rescue

Vicki Meakin and Suzanne Emson preparing the breakfasts

Inside the horses mobile home for the next 8 days

Jimmy Wheeler dealing with the first drama with the brakes

Colin positions the pole

Mick prepares his legs

The team at the start - Start time 09.00 hours, 21st June 2011

Competing with the holiday traffic

On through Cornwall

Escort riders depart with Ambulance after successful first changeover

The A30 stretches ahead

The staff at Penzance Tesco provide breakfast, bucket rattlers and a warm welcome

Paul and Lyn Burns sort out harnesses

On through Devon, north of Exeter

Changing horses - In the rain again

Into the dry at the end of a shift

Charlie prepares to depart

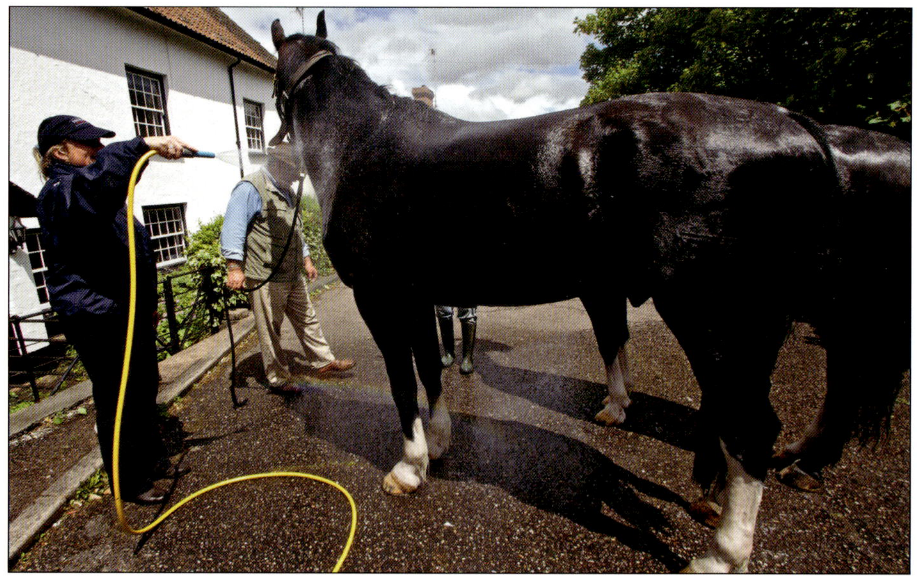

Wash down at the end of a leg

Steeply into Somerset with the stallions

Charlie and Debbie ready for the off

John Davies - On foot for once

NEMO ME IMPUNE LACESSIT
ORION

Matt briefs the Mayor of Taunton

On their own initiative, Tom and Alex raise £354 from their school - Queen's College Taunton

Queen's College Taunton schoolchildren greet the ambulance

DAY 3 - SHEPTON MALLET TO NEWENT

Paul, The Mayor of Bath and Francis at breakfast time in Victoria Park

Escort protection outside Bath, thanks to Dick Lovett BMW

Peaceful Wiltshire with the Hackneys in harness

British greetings at Chippenham Ambulance Station - Jacks' paramedic base

Finn Bruce and Matt star on TV

Matt explains his arm injuries to inquisitive children, while everyone enjoyed delicious hospitality!

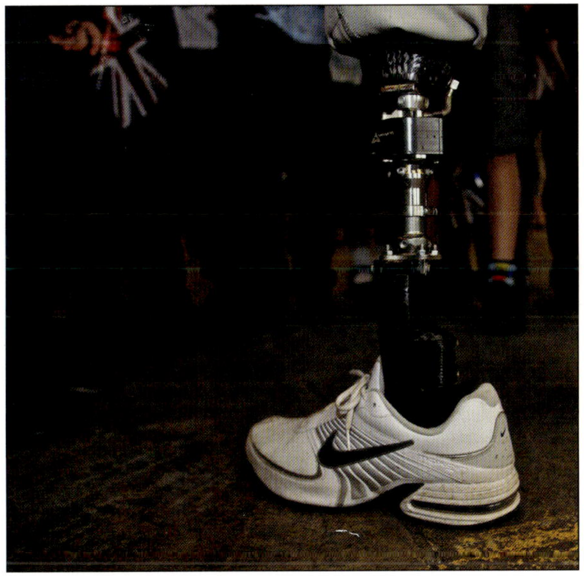

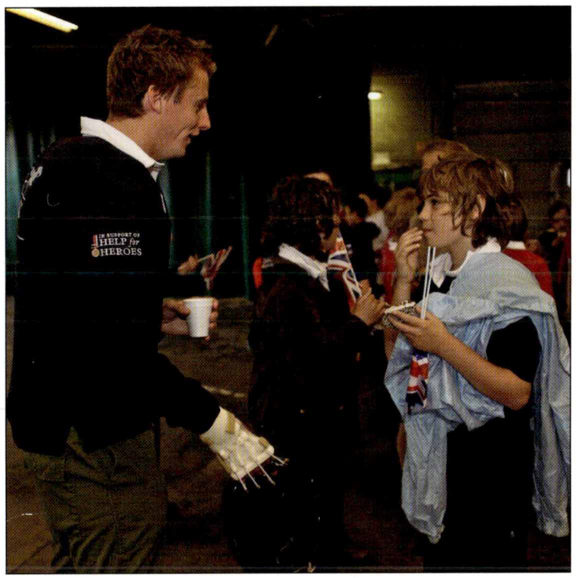

Francis engages the young

Great Western Ambulance Service welcomes 'an older ambulance' to Chippenham

The ambulance and escort riders climb Malmesbury High Street

Cheers from The Nursery, now an hour late

John with Shirley Collier and friend lead the collection team

Keen young supporters

Jacks with sons Adam and Harry - expert collectors by now

The crowds turn out in Malmesbury with The Abbey in the backdrop

Collections on the run

John demonstrates the art of pub collections

Bear Grylls rides escort in Cirencester

Bear and Mark Todd

Bear and Mark join the escorts and RLC soldiers from South Cerney in the Market Square, Cirencester

Serena shares the joke

Into Gloucestershire as a storm gathers

DAY 4 - PRESTON CROSS TO WARRINGTON

Some of the Tarporley team

Jacks and Colin gratefully receive another cheque

Danny shows off his leg

Cadets gather round eager to learn

Ian Sawyer and Colin address young enthusiasts of Shrewsbury

Onwards into Cheshire

The patient Tarporley supporters soaked to the skin

The rear convoy car provides protection in the wet

Andy Taylor - 1am changeover

Andy Spatcher, night leader, reaches for the harness

One of a thousand kisses

Shrewsbury dignitaries make a donation with the Mayor

With fundraisers outside a Whitchurch country house

Dusk in Tarporley centre

Juggernauts in the night test the noble horses

John Lapper, a night crew stalwart

Food and shelter for horses on the move

Uplifting midnight greetings from Wigan residents

The Mayor of Wigan welcomes Gareth Ely and Danny

DAY 5 - ASHTON IN MAKERFIELD TO PENRITH

En-route to Lancaster

Lancaster dignitaries show their support from the Castle

Jane - The challenge mascot

Mounted escorts in front of Lancaster Castle

Ace pathfinder and changeover selector Phil studies the map

Paddy - Phil's loyal companion

Horsebox crew on the move

End of shift

Sue, Debbie and Charlie

The Lake District hills loom ahead

The Bowman team tackles the Shap ascent

At the top of Shap - A rewarding welcome and a large cheque from the eventers of Cumbria

Professional carriage racer Barnaby charges his team of four up to the summit of Shap, the first time since his father completed the climb in 1972

Tilly Bruce - HHH's amazing Girl Friday

Barnaby Bowman - One of the family world champion drivers

Mist and fog close in towards the summit of Shap

DAY 6 - CARLISLE TO GLASGOW

Crossing the historic border

The night team - Jimmy, Andy, Gary and John

Andy Taylor and his Shire Heavies

Sorting a tangle of leathers

R & R

Ken Ruthven and his guest team head north from Gretna

Toby Gordon on a mission

A loyal greeting from Colin's family in Dumbarton

DAY 7 - DUMBARTON TO FORT WILLIAM

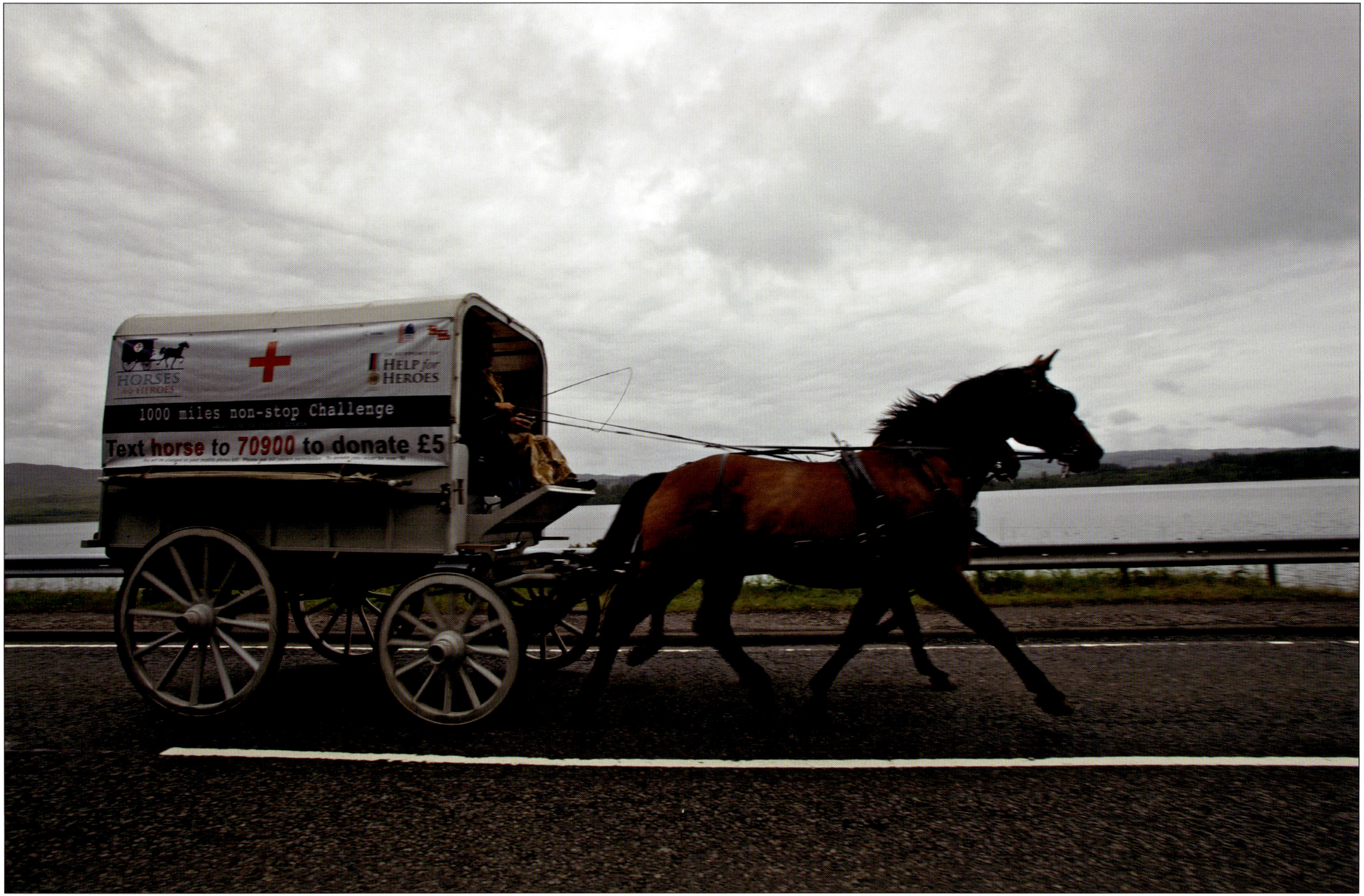

McInnes pair step out along Loch Awe

Beauty beside Loch Awe

Colourful young collectors

Onwards and northwards into The Highlands

John making up valuable time

View from within

Matt takes a well-earned power nap

Closing on our destination

John takes a leg maintenance stop

James chats to BLESMA members who travelled miles to meet us at North Connell

The steel Connell Bridge towers over the ambulance team

Matt takes in the sunset

Jacks and John push to the summit of Commando Point, Spean Bridge

Time to reflect at The Commando Memorial

Colin - Our 'resident Scotsman' surveys his homeland

Forward into the darkening night

Hi from Phil!

Heading north from Inverness on the A9

Thanks to Mitsubishi for the escort lead

Bernie Tidmarsh shaping a shoe

Leaving The Black Isle for Easter Ross

Final stretch for Moulton's Big Red Beast!

The Provest of Inverness chats to resident Colin

Kaz, Mick and Sue delight some junior jockeys

Guy's invaluable towing wagon - The mainstay of over 30 events

Boutique branding in Tain

Photography and filming vehicle kindly supplied by Land Rover

DAY 9 - HELMSDALE TO JOHN O'GROATS

The sun rises over Beriedale Braes

The Shires heavies lean into their collars and steadily conquer the famed gradients of the Beriedale Braes

A huge school's welcome turns out in Wick

Wick's worst weather

Oh dear! But the only one en-route - 8th day fatigue

Four up. John's and Colin's last leg into Caithness

13-mile countdown

Phil Scott was young once!

Happiness from the dedicated support team

Mission completed in 8 days and 7 hours - An amazing record-breaking achievement.

Lord Lieutenant of Caithness congratulates our wounded heroes

We've made it - James and Guy share Jacks' emotion

Oli shares celebration bubbles with Mick

Henry, Charlie and Paul relax and enjoy the joke

Euphoric success

Phantom photography

Our smiling wounded team stands as a symbol for all seriously wounded servicemen. They show what can be overcome with their unique determination and fighting spirit

POST-CHALLENGE

Best Western sponsors presenting trophy for the Best Western Horses Help Heroes Stakes

Winning the race at Goodwood

Royal Berkshire Show, Newbury

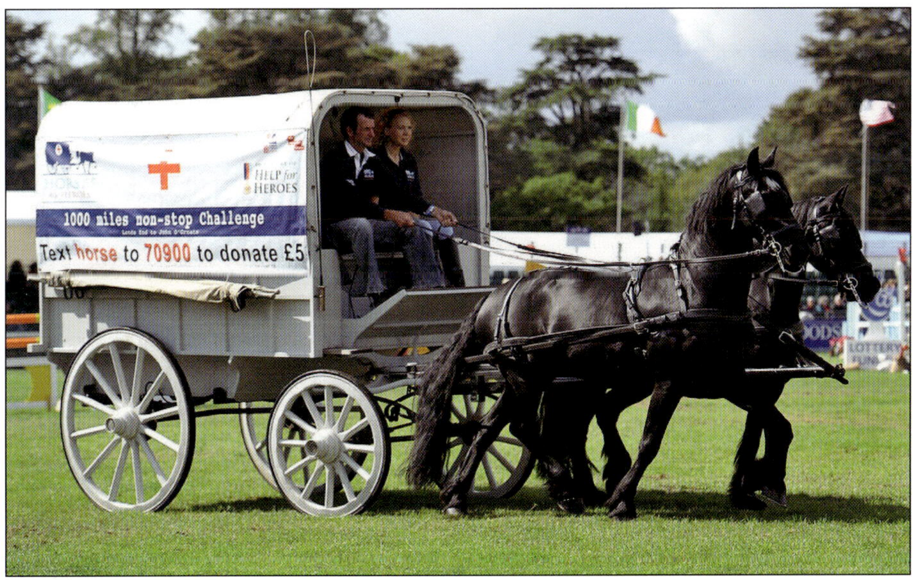

Fidelity Blenheim International Horse Trial

Cartier International Polo - The winning English team - Nacho Gonzalez, Luke Tomlinson, Jane Beim, Mark Tomlinson - show brilliant support for the cause after beating Brazil

Organisers at Badminton Sponsored Ride

A united pair in front of Badminton House

HORSES
help HEROES

The Horses Help Heroes campaign has received generous help and support from many hundreds of people across the UK. Listed below are some of their names (others will have been overlooked, for which we apologise). There will be hundreds more who contribute, and we thank everyone most sincerely for their kindness to the fundraising.

The campaign continues: www.horseshelpheroes.org.uk

HORSES HELP HEROES CHALLENGE PARTICIPANTS

Vince Almond - Driver
Francis Atkinson - Wounded carriage and escort driver
Jane Boswell - Veterinary Surgeon
Finn Bruce - PR / Marketing (Bell Pottinger)
Tilly Bruce - Groom
Arthur Bunce - Farrier
Paul Burns - Wounded carriage and escort driver
Kim Cobbold - PR / Marketing
Debbie Cunningham - Driver, HGV, Groom
John Davies - Carriage driver; Horse owner
Adam De Silva - Still Photographer / RPM
Sophie Dyke - Groom
Richard Dyke
Fahd El Tawil - Escort Vehicle Driver
Jacks El Tawil - Carriage driver; Horse owner
Gareth Ely - Carriage driver, HGV
James Emson - Convoy Commander
Mick Foulds - Wounded carriage and escort driver
Sue Foulds - Riding horses
Marcus Giles - Veterinary Surgeon
Toby Gordon
Colin Hamilton - Wounded carriage and escort driver
Danny Holmes - Wounded carriage and escort driver
John Lapper - Driver, HGV
David Lewis - Escort Vehicle Driver
David Lloyd - Veterinary Surgeon
Sandy Love - Veterinary Surgeon
Jeremy Mantell - Veterinary Surgeon
Justin Mather - Escort Vehicle Driver
Henry Meakin - Chairman
Vicki Meakin - Reception Committees, Fundraising
Oliver Meakin
Guy Parry - Merchandising Trailer
Lyn Peters - Groom & Escort vehicle driver
Charlie Reeves - Carriage driver; Horse owner
Martin Robbins - Movie Photographer / RPM
John Sandford-Hart - Wounded carriage and escort driver
Lesley Smith - Merchandising Trailer
Andy Spatcher - Carriage driver; Horse owner
Andy Taylor - Carriage driver
Steph Thomas - Groom
Bernie Tidmarsh - Farrier
Toby Turner - Farrier
Tim Villiers - Deputy Convoy Commander
Jimmy Wheeler - Mr Fix-it!
Matt Wilson - Wounded carriage and escort driver

HORSES HELP HEROES - DRIVING AND RIDING

Jacks El Tawil's
Molly and Rosie: Black, Fresian, Mares

John Davies
Mole and Alby: Friesian, Stallions
Pascal and Romeo: Gelding, Gelderlander
Theo and Kai: Gelding, Gelderlanders
Winston and Pelle: Black, Friesians, Stallions

Charlie Reeves
George and Soli: Bay, Friesian/Hackney cross, Geldings

Andy Spatcher's
Badwins Rosario: Bay, Hackney/Friesian cross
Florence: Black, French Trotting Mare
Nibos and Cirrius: Black, Gelding
Woodleigh Charlie and Ponteous: Hackney Bay geldings

Andy Taylor
Billy and Horace – Shires

RIDING HORSES - ESCORTS

Mick Foulds - Kaz

Craig and Serena Dolby - Patches: Cob

Donna - Charlie: Cob

HORSES HELP HEROES KEY SUPPORTERS

HRH The Duke of Cambridge

Claire Balding
Simon Bazalgette
James Blunt
General Sir Richard Dannatt, GCB, CBE, MC
Frankie Dettori
William Fox Pitt
Goldie
Bear Grylls
General Lord Guthrie
Chris Harper
Nicky Henderson
Carl Hester
Charlie Longsdon
Alice Plunkett
Emma Spencer
Tim Stockdale
Sir Michael Stoute
Kevin Swift
Mark Todd
Mike Tucker
Michael Whitaker

HORSES HELP HEROES MAJOR SUPPORTERS

Vince Almond
Arabella Arkwright
Victor Beeching
Mel Beeching
Simon Brookes-Ward
Tilly Bruce
Anthony Cane
John and Dawn Cleland
Earl & Countess of Caernarvon
Evelyn Cameron
Barney Clifford
Sir Malcolm Cohquhoun
Helen Cole
Harriet Collins
Jim Corbett
Robert Cudmore
Louise Daly
Peter Daresbury
Andrew Dixey
Duke of Beaufort
Robert Eddy
Ian Farquhar
Andrew Franklin
Ed Gretton
Margaret Gurney
Alistair and Annette Hammond-Chambers
Christopher Joll
Ginny Keene
Kempton Park
Kirkland and Ellis
John Lovering
Peter Lovett
Lord March
Toby Marshall
Richard Matson
Nigel Meakin
Peter Meakin
Cherry Mitchell
Anne Monks
Kim Morris
Vanessa Naider
Hugh Pitman
Jack Ramsdon
Linda Ramsdon
David Reid Scott
Zoe Rucker
Lord & Lady Rowallan
Maureen Ryder-Gordon
Sara Shore
Robert Shore
Jonno Spence
Lord Strathnaver
The Lovering Charitable Trust
Hugh Thomas
John Tinsley
Mark Todd
Simon Tomlinson
Claire Tomlinson
Jane Tuckwell
Mike Tucker
Andrew Tucker
Greville Vernon
Richard Vernon
James Vernon
Mike Wilson
David Woode
Mark Todd

HORSES HELP HEROES OFFICIAL BODIES AND CORPORATE SUPPORTERS

Aberdeen Asset Management
A C Nurden Ltd
Aintree Racecourse
Aldon Horse Trials
Arnold Clark
Asda
Badminton Horse Trials
Beaufort Hunt
Beaufort Polo Club
Best Western Hotels
Bickenhall Horse Trials
Blenheim International Horse Trials
British Dressage
British Driving Society
British Dressage
British Eventing
British Horse Society
British Military Tatoo
British Show Eventing
British Show Jumping
Cascade Productions
Coniston Corporate
Chester Racecourse
Coutts
Devizes Trailers
Dick Lovett Specialist Cars
Epsom Racecourse
Golden Bottle Trust
Goodwood Racecourse
Guards Polo Club
Highclere Castle
Hurlingham Polo Association
iCap
Investec
Kempton Park
Kingfisher
Lowther Horse Trials
Master of Foxhounds Association
Sainsbury's
Smith and Williamson
System Signs Ltd
Tesco
The Jockey Club
The Pony Club
Towmaster

HORSES HELP HEROES SUPPORTERS

Emily Ackroyd
Ed Addington
Sheila Aiken
Jo Aldridge
Hugh Anderson
Helen Apperley
Helen Appleby
Violet Arkwright
Mr & Mrs Ashworth
Charlie Aylesford
Garry Bain
Anna Lisa Balding
Brian Ball
Russell Barker
Karen Barker
Vicki Bateman
Lee Bateson
Justin Beckett
Edward Belcher
Anne Binns
Paul Birket-Wendes
Shelley Booth
George Bowman
Barnaby Bowman
Box and Seal
Sue-Gay Bridgeman
Fiona Britton
Clare Bromfield
Jon Burton
Shirley Burton
Pat Calderbank
Anthony Cane
Ray Cargill
Chris Carver
Siobhan Carver
Sacha Cauwels-Wigan
Sarah Clegg
Annette Clarke
Jack Clyne
Maureen Coghill
Joe Coleman
Shirley Collier
Oliver Colville MP
Sally Cooper
Faith Cox
Countrywide, Ludlow
Julie Crew
Linda Crocott
Peter Currie
Deborah Custance-Baker
Louise Daly
Charlie Dalziel
Richard Dannatt
Merlin Dernie
Devizes Trailers
Mr & Mrs Dewhurst
Tina Dickinson
Lionel Digby
Serena Dolby
Craig Dolby
Anne Donn
Hendrik du Toit - Investec
Judy and Peter Duckworth
Richard Durham
Jon Dylon
Barbara Eaglesfield
Kit Ebben
Mo Edwards
Cynthia Fletcher
Peter Ford
Isabel Forrest
Anita Foulsham
William Fox-Pitt
Sarah Frost
James Fuller
Lucy Fuller
Thea Garwood
Julian Gray
James Gray MP
Stephanie Grayson
Judy Green
Mr & Mrs Griffiths
Bear Grylls
Jean Gunn
Lord Guthrie
Andrew Hamilton
Sarah Harden
Edward Harding-Newman
William Hartley Russell
Diana Hardy
Helen Harris
Harry - logo designer
David Hart
Hartbury College, Gloucester
Luke Havill
June Haydon
Angela Heatherington
Alan & Tricia Hedley
Nicky Henderson
Carl Hester
Robert & Mrs Hewson
Kathleen Hill
Lindsay Hill
Philip Holder
Alex Horsfall
Horse and Country TV
Dan Hughes
Helen Humphreys
Shaun Hunt
Jessica Hutchinson
Rupert Hutchinson Smith
Catriona Innes
Claire Jakerman
Charlie Johnson
David Jones - Ferrier
Stephanie Kill
Chris Kirby
Adrian Lander
Penny Lander
Julian Lander
Richard Lanni
Rosey Lediard
Catherine Lumsden
Sophie Lynsey
Stacie MacDonald
Mannington Equestrian
Bev Marmont
Lyn Marriott-Lodge
Maryculter Driving Centre
Charlie Massey - Coffee man
George Mathewson
Roy Matthews
Clare McDonald
Diana McDonald
Kim McGarva
Ewan McInnes
Julie McKeivor
Bill McLean
Peter McLean
Sheila McNeill

Gary Medlicott
Katherine Mellor
Simon Miller
Stuart Mills
Tricia Morris
Susan Morrison
Jessica Moseley
Jim Mullock
Family Munro Ferguson
Catriona Murray
Jennifer Nelligan
Mike Nimmo
Roland Notley
Richard Nunneley
P Ormond
Alice O'Neil
Duncan Paget
John Parker
Jill Pay
Hugh Pitman
Roger Plowden
Alice Plunkett
Evelyn Pottie
Fiona Powell
Adrian Pratt
Charlotte Rasmussen
Matt Read
Sandra Reid
Dan Richards
Aileen Roberts
Andy Robertshaw
Mark Rogers
Bill Ross
Clive Rushton-Green
Alex Salmond MSP
Margaret Sanderson
Gareth Saunders
Ian Sawers
Mark & Amanda Scott
Roger Shepherd
Jack Shortman
Peter Sidebottom
Chris Simmons
Slade of Devizes
Darren Slade
Anne Smith
Rupert Smith

Martin Snow
Angela Spatcher
Spencer - Photographer
Bill Spiegleberg
Helen Steele
Sue Stewart
James Stewart
Andrew Stewart-Mills
Tim Stockdale
Margaret Stokes
Lord Strathclyde
Ellie Sulter
Brian Suter
Linda Swaine
Kevin Swift
Jane Symonds
Jane Symonds
James Tanner
Kirkland Tellwright
James Thompson
Catherine Titherleigh
Jessica Tomblin
Lynn Townsend
Mike Tucker
Andrew Tucker
Mrs G Tudor
Caroline Turner
Jonathan Turner
Kate Varley
Wadswick Country Store
Kay Walton
Helen Watkins
Janette Watson
Louise Welch
Julian Western
Isabelle Westerling
Douglas & Lucinda Weymouth
Hazel Woodbridge
Philip Yea

PHOTOGRAPHY

Principle photographer Adam De Silva - RPM.
Other contributing photographers
Steve Bardens
Patrick Dolan
Chris Raphael

Matt Sills
Spencer McPhearson
Phil Stevens
Other image supplied by Horses Help Heroes

HORSES HELP HEROES MAIN SPONSORS

RPM
Steve Bardens
Geraldine Buhrkohl
Adam De Silva
Joe Dizon
Patrick Dolan
Lee Farrant
Ross Gosling
Damian James
Dermot McQuaid
Chris Raphael
Martin Robbins
Gee Sambrook-Smith
Carl Smith
Dave Squires
Rob Wilson

BELL POTTINGER
Lord Bell
Sue Farr
Luke Chauveau
June Selby
Luke Havill
Finn Bruce
Daisy Barran

BEST WESTERN HOTELS
Mark Smith
Fahd El Tawil

NATURAL ANIMAL FEEDS
Richard Cleeve

DIAGEO

HORSES HELP HEROES COMMITTEE MEMBERS

Henry Meakin (Chairman)
James Emson (Deputy)

Fhad El Tawil
Jackie El Tawil
Katie Gordon
Toby Gordon
Harry Meakin
Oli Meakin
Vicki Meakin
Guy Parry
Tim Villiers